A Manager's Guide to the Long-Term Preservation of Electronic Documents

A Manager's Guide to the Long-Term Preservation of Electronic Documents

Neil Pitman and
Alan Shipman

Business Information

First published in the UK in 2008

by
BSI
389 Chiswick High Road
London W4 4AL

British Library Cataloguing in Publication Data
A catalogue record for this book is available from the British Library

ISBN 978-0-580-61351-7

Typeset in Optima and Minion by Helius, Brighton and Rochester
Printed in Great Britain by MPG Books, Bodmin, Cornwall

Contents

1 The digital preservation problem 1

   1.1 *The need for document preservation* 1

   1.2 *Defining 'long-term'* 2

   1.3 *Preservable digital documents* 3

   1.4 *Aspects of preservation* 3

   1.5 *Preservation challenges* 5

   1.6 *Preservation approaches* 8

   1.7 *Digital document preservation policy* 14

2 Retention periods 17

   2.1 *Definitions* 17

   2.2 *Principles of retention periods* 18

   2.3 *Implementation* 24

3 Standards-based archival formats 31

   3.1 *Characteristics of archival formats* 31

   3.2 *Standards bodies* 35

   3.3 *Non-digital archival format* 36

   3.4 *Digital archival formats* 39

   3.5 *Guidance for specific document categories* 59

4 Storage media 63

   4.1 *Paper* 64

4.2	*Microfilm*	68
4.3	*Magnetic tape*	71
4.4	*Optical disk*	74
4.5	*On-line storage*	77
4.6	*Summary*	80
5	Metadata	81
5.1	*Metadata in long-term preservation of digital documents*	81
5.2	*The purpose of metadata*	82
5.3	*Metadata formats*	83
5.4	*Metadata schemas*	84
5.5	*Custom schemas*	86
5.6	*Data standards*	86
5.7	*UK Government*	87
5.8	*Metadata location*	87
5.9	*Technical metadata*	88
5.10	*Other relevant standards*	88
6	Archive creation and maintenance	89
6.1	*Core concepts*	89
6.2	*OAIS functional model*	93
7	Related standards and publications	97
7.1	*The OAIS model*	97
7.2	*Records management*	99

7.3 *Document management*   100

7.4 *Legal admissibility*   101

7.5 *PDF/A*   101

8   References   103

Annex A – Policy document   105

The digital preservation problem

1

1.1 The need for document preservation

In the modern era, digital documents are being created at an unprecedented rate. At the same time, increasing regulation is placing ever more stringent requirements on the need for retention of documents over a long period of time.

Examples of digital documents
- MS Office documents
- PDF documents
- TIFF and JPEG image files
- HTML web files
- Email documents and attachments
- MS Project files
- Computer Aided Design (CAD) files
- Voice and video files

This leaves commercial and government organizations with a new challenge: how can digital documents be reliably preserved for decades or even centuries when digital formats change regularly?

Historically, paper and microfilm have provided the solution to the long-term preservation of documents. Whilst these non-digital solutions are certainly still an option, increasingly there is a business need to provide digital archives allowing convenient electronic access to those documents for decades or even centuries.

The rapid change in file formats and storage media creates a risk that in the future digital documents either may not be readable at all or may be readable but without confidence that the document appearance or behaviour matches that of the document when it was first created.

It should be pointed out that 'digital preservation' is not the same as 'backup'. Whilst backup systems can be used to recover information that has been 'lost' from a computer system, they typically are used to recover a specific system wholesale, rather than to retain information over the long term.

1.2 Defining 'long-term'

Whilst 'long-term' is traditionally defined in terms of numbers of

---

Definition: long-term

A period of time long enough for there to be concern about the impacts of changing technologies, including support for new media and data formats, and of a changing user community, on the information being held in a repository. This period extends into the indefinite future.

Typically, this may equate to between 5 and 10 years – shorter for some systems.

---

years, in the context of digital document preservation 'long-term' is concerned with the lifespan of the document's technical format rather than some arbitrary period such as 15, 50 or 500 years.

1.3 Preservable digital documents

There currently exists a wide range of digital document formats ranging from simple text documents to images to complex 'documents' such as a Microsoft Project file or AutoCAD drawing. The scope of this guide extends to all types of document for which suitable mechanisms are currently available for long-term preservation.

It should be understood that some documents may not be fully preservable with current mechanisms. Later chapters will fully explain the issues, but as an initial example, whilst it will be possible to preserve printed versions of various views of a Microsoft Project file, there are significant challenges in maintaining its behaviour over the long term.

1.4 Aspects of preservation

There are a number of aspects to the preservation of digital documents. When planning a strategy for preservation, consideration needs to be given to which of these preservation aspects are required and indeed, which aspects may not even be possible to preserve for certain document types.

1.4.1 Content

Preservation of content refers to retaining the textual and image content of a file without regard to the precise formatting of the document. Often this can be provided by a text dump of the original file.

Example

Retaining a complex spreadsheet as a text file – this preserves the data from the spreadsheet, but not the various formulae and cross-references.

1.4.2 Visual appearance

Fidelity of appearance refers to maintaining an equivalent of the *visual* (such as a paper printout) version of the document – including images. The preservation may be colour, greyscale or bi-tonal.

Example

Retaining a complex spreadsheet as an image file – this preserves the visual perception of the spreadsheet, but not data or formulae/cross-references.

1.4.3 Structure and interactivity

Documents often contain structural and interactive elements such as bookmarks, tables of contents and internal hyperlinks.

Example

Retaining a complex spreadsheet in its original form will preserve the visual perception of the spreadsheet, as well as the data or formulae/cross-references.

Key point

When planning preservation, an analysis of the preservation requirements for each class of document is an essential prerequisite.

1.5 Preservation challenges

1.5.1 File formats

The biggest challenge to long-term preservation is that presented by the choice of the document file format. New, often proprietary, file formats arise with new versions of word processors and other office programs. Whilst continual conversion between formats may seem to be a solution, each time a file is converted to a new format there is a risk of some loss of fidelity whether in the precise document appearance or the interactive behaviour. Computer Aided Design (CAD) systems are well known for not providing backward compatibility, requiring frequent updating to ensure accessibility.

It should be accepted that there are currently only a relatively small number of file formats suitable for long-term archiving, each of which has its own unique advantages and disadvantages. Chapter 3 of this guide discusses archival file formats in some detail.

1.5.2 Storage media

Historically the greatest preservation challenge has been regarded as that of storage media. With an e-preservation strategy, ensuring that the electronic file (e.g. the stream of bits that make up the representation) is maintained is straightforward. In the current era, well-established practices exist for backup procedures and strategies exist for media refreshment (including copy verification).

Chapter 4 of this guide discusses strategies for storage covering both operational models and choice of media, ranging from paper and microfilm to various types of electronic media.

Key point
Long-term preservation should be distinguished from backup and data archiving systems, which are purely concerned with the preservation of bit streams, rather than aiming to ensure accessibility of the documents and related metadata.

1.5.3 Metadata

It is critical that document metadata[1] is preserved alongside the document itself. In many modern systems, metadata is stored in a database that references the document. Requirements for the preservation of metadata in association with the document should thus be included within the preservation strategy.

It is also important to note that the contents of the document metadata may change during preservation. Whilst it is important to 'fix' certain metadata over time, other metadata (such as details of any file format conversions that have occurred) may need to be added from time to time.

For long-term preservation purposes, the metadata must be stored either in the document itself (e.g. using the XMP model for PDF/A) or as a separate external file with a maintained link.

> **Key point**
> When planning preservation, it is highly recommended that each document class has one or more XML schemas associated with it, either standardized schema such as Dublin Core or custom extension schemas.

---

[1]Metadata is defined as 'data describing the context, content and structure of records and their management through time' (ISO 15489).

In addition, file provenance and history information needs to be recorded using either XMP or equivalent. Chapter 5 of this guide discusses strategies for metadata definitions and preservation.

1.5.4 Documentation

Documenting the precise formats used and the semantics of metadata elements for preserved documents can easily be forgotten. Where long-term preservation is required, documentation – which itself needs to be preserved – can be used in the future to identify and display the digital documents in an authentic manner.

1.5.5 Compound objects

Compound documents such as documents with embedded components and emails with attachments deserve special consideration. Subclauses 3.5.2 and 3.5.3 provide specific guidance for emails and web pages. The actual strategy implemented by an organization will depend upon the specific requirements and in particular the approved retention periods. Often, a mixed strategy will be appropriate.

1.6 Preservation approaches

A number of different approaches to preservation are possible, each with advantages and disadvantages. The following are approaches currently in use, and a strategy should employ one or more of these techniques.

1.6.1 Technology preservation

This approach requires the preservation of hardware and software information systems in order to ensure access to digital documents over their retention period. It is essentially a 'do nothing' approach. This approach is typically a viable long-term solution only where one or two anticipated technology changes are expected over the appropriate retention period (say between 5 and 15 years).

Advantages

- It may be an inexpensive option where minimal retrievals are required, e.g. do nothing.
- It does not require any format conversions of the digital documents.

Disadvantages

- It typically becomes increasingly difficult and costly over time.
- There is a potential for lack of user familiarity with ageing applications/technology.
- It may involve ageing and/or obsolete storage media which may be difficult to maintain.
- It may pose metadata issues.

1.6.2 Emulation

This approach requires the availability of systems that mimic the functionality of older hardware and software (operating systems and document authoring or viewing software). Individual electronic documents are retained in their original format.

> **Example**
> Documents created using older versions of Microsoft Word could be run on Windows 3.1 using Virtual PC.

Advantages

- The emulating systems can run on current operational environments.
- They can integrate easily with existing systems.
- Wholesale format conversions are not required.

Disadvantages

- The user needs to be aware of all formats/technologies that require mimicking software.
- It relies on the availability of suitable mimicking systems.
- It raises potential software licensing issues.
- There is a potential for lack of user familiarity with ageing applications.
- There is a risk of potential Y2K-type software failures.
- It involves multiple points of failure.

1.6.3 Conversion/migration

This requires the periodic transfer of digital material from one format to another, usually from the format used by a superseded version of an authoring program to a newer one.

Example

Documents created using older versions of Microsoft Word are converted to the latest Word format, using a Microsoft batch processing tool.

Advantages

- It runs on current operational environments.
- It integrates easly with existing systems.

Disadvantages

- There is a risk of inadvertent alteration of the document during conversion: the more complex the record, the higher the risk.
- It may require knowledge of the identity of the original software authoring tools associated with each electronic document.
- It is a continuous and relatively frequent process, based on technology changes.

1.6.4 Encapsulation

This combines several elements to create a new digital object, usually encapsulated in XML containers. The contained objects may include metadata along with the digital document in both its original format and converted format versions.

Example

A single XML file can act as a container for the original version of a Word file, together with one or more copies of the file stored in other formats such as OOXML or PDF/A. The XML file would also contain document metadata. Binary files such as Word documents may be stored within the XML file using base-64 encoding.

Advantages

- There is a single archive object, which reduces the risk of separation of metadata and the different versions of the document.
- By keeping the original along with converted formats, risk of document loss or alteration is minimized.

Disadvantages

- The archive XML package may require more complex processing to create and retrieve the digital document than that required for other preservation approaches.

1.6.5 Conversion to standard formats

This approach transforms records into formats following recognized standards such as XML, ASCII or PDF/A at some point during the creation or storage of the digital document. Typically, conversion to the standard format is performed, sometimes under automated system control, when the document is stored within an electronic document management system. Conversion may also be part of a record declaration process. Chapter 3 covers standard formats in detail.

Advantages

- It is easy to demonstrate authenticity when required.
- It will always run on current operational environments as a standard format is being used.
- It decreases the dependence on specific hardware and software.
- It is future-proof, as the internal format is fully specified as an ISO (or other) standard.

Disadvantages

- There is a small risk of inadvertent alteration of the document during conversion to the standard format.
- Requires procedures to be followed during the creation/declaration of a digital document.

- Choosing the appropriate standard format is not always a straight-forward process.
- Lifespan depends on longevity of the selected standard.
- It can entail loss of functionality in converted documents.
- It can be difficult with complex compound files.

1.7 Digital document preservation policy

1.7.1 Policy

As part of an organization's information strategy, a policy document for digital document preservation should be produced.

The policy document should contain the following sections.

Section	Content	Reference in this guide
1. Scope	Defines the area of business and types of document covered by the policy	—
2. Legal, regulatory and best practice requirements	Specifies the requirements for document retention as defined by relevant statutes and best practice	Chapter 2
3. Detailed retention schedule	Defines the retention period for each document class covered by the policy	Chapter 2

4. Archive model	Describes the overall preservation model, covering the ingestion, storage, administration and retrieval of archived documents	Chapter 6
5. Storage media	Specifies the range of storage media and media management practices used for long-term preservation	Chapter 4
6. File formats	Specifies the set of file formats to be used and the relationship between source file formats and archive formats	Chapter 3
7. Metadata standards	Describes the XML schema used to record metadata for each document class	Chapter 5
8. Responsibilities	Allocates specific functional responsibility for policy implementation	—
9. Preservation planning	Defines the policy review schedule	1.7.2

1.7.2 Policy review schedule

The ever-changing technical and regulatory landscapes require periodic reviews to determine whether any change in policy is required. An annual review is advised, covering in particular the following:

- assessment of any new or changed legal or regulatory requirements – there may be a requirement to take into account changes to retention periods in the light of new or updated legislation, or of requirements from industry regulators;
- a review of new storage media technologies – existing storage media may need to be extended or replaced, to meet new business needs;
- a review of new standard file formats.

Retention periods

2

Even outside of an extensive electronic records management system (ERMS), long-term preservation requires the adoption of certain ERMS principles, in particular the definition of retention periods and metadata standards for different classes of document. The approaches are well documented in various ERMS standards, and specific guidance on retention periods can be obtained from the Record Management Society and other sources that are referenced.

2.1 Definitions

Formal definitions of terms used in records management processes are included in ISO 15489, *Information and documentation. Records management.* This international standard defines the term 'record' and specifies the major stages in the management of these records.

Definition: record
Information created, received and maintained as evidence and information by an organization or person, in pursuance of legal obligations or in the transaction of business (from ISO 15489).

ISO 15489 identifies the following stages that should be implemented to ensure a good records management system:

- policies and responsibilities;
- principles of records management programmes;
- design and implementation of a records management system;
- records management processes and controls;
- monitoring and auditing.

This chapter will look at the principles of retention periods and will discuss how they should be implemented in an electronic environment.

2.2 Principles of retention periods

2.2.1 Record life cycles

The main phases of a record's life cycle are as follows:

- creation – including drafting, version control and storage;
- disposition – allocating and implementing retention periods;
- appraisal – determining the action to be taken at the end of the retention period;
- preservation – retaining the record in the long term, typically for historical purposes;
- disposal – removing the record from storage.

The disposition phase is one of the major functions of a records management system. This phase is used to identify, control and implement the management of retention periods. Such retention periods may be required by an individual or business for one or more of the following purposes:

- legal and regulatory requirements;
- business requirements;
- cost management;
- personal information retention as required by the Data Protection Act;
- legal discovery and other retrieval purposes.

Each of these points is described in detail in 2.2.2 to 2.2.6.

2.2.2 Legal and regulatory requirements

There are many and varied legal and regulatory requirements for retaining records for particular periods of time. These requirements will vary, depending upon the country within which the individual or business is operating, and depending upon the policies of any regulatory bodies applicable to the individual or business.

In all cases (with the possible exception of the Data Protection Act 1998), all legal and regulatory requirements will define minimum retention periods (records must be retained for at least ...). Thus, there are no legal or regulatory requirements that require disposal after certain periods of time.

Example: legal retention requirements

For organizations in the financial sector, one applicable legal require-ment is documented in the Money Laundering Regulations 2003, which includes (amongst many other requirements) the need to keep 'satisfactory evidence of identity' of the applicant. In the case of the establishment of identity, the Regulations require that appropriate records are retained for 5 years.

Example: regulatory retention requirements

For organizations in the financial sector, the major regulatory body is the Financial Services Authority (FSA). The FSA also imposes specific reten-tion requirements to complement the Money Laundering Regulations, including the requirement to keep records of disclosures and informa-tion not acted upon to be retained for a similar retention period.

2.2.3 Business requirements

All businesses will have requirements to retain a record of their activi-ties for a period of time. The actual retention time required by the busi-ness will need to be decided, taking into account the needs of all the business units within the organization.

Often, business retention periods will need to be defined on the basis of a risk assessment. Business managers will need to assess the effect of destroying records after a particular period of time. Such decisions will also need to be revisited on a regular basis, taking into account any changes to business risk that are identified.

Example

A business that supplies temporary staff to its customers will need to retain signed-off timesheets in order to raise the appropriate invoices. It will also need to retain them until customers have accepted and settled the invoices. There is thus a business need to retain timesheets until the invoice is paid. (There may be other business requirements that require a longer retention period.)

Risk assessment

Typically, building records are retained for a number of years, in order to deal with any issues related to the demonstration that building regulations and planning consents had been complied with. Businesses also considered that retaining records for the limitations period would cover any issues around latent defects and building maintenance. However, recent cases of asbestosis claims by people who had been working in an affected building have been made after much longer time periods. This issue has led to an increase in retention periods to retain building details for use in the event of a claim.

2.2.4 Cost management

Over the last few years, there has been much debate on the relation between the costs of retaining information and the cost of destruction.

With electronic storage, many business managers consider that the cost of retaining a document is negligible. Such factors as 'electronic storage is cheap' and 'I don't have time to sort out my records' have led to an increasing volume of records retained in electronic storage. This issue is particularly true for email systems, where in-boxes are being used by employees as their own record store.

IT managers have recently become aware of this increasing issue, which is resulting in the requirement for additional storage space, longer backup cycles, increased business needs for '24/7' operation, longer search times and slower retrieval times.

In some organizations, this issue with email has led to the implementation of a policy of 'deletion after x months', with x ranging from 1 to 6. Such a policy is applied globally, irrespective of the types of document involved. This policy, in turn and without due diligence of individual recipients of email, can lead to a high risk of the loss of important business records. The policy has resulted, in some organizations, in a lack of confidence in the electronic record storage systems. Some individuals have countered this issue by printing and filing all important records, without considering the environmental and business efficiency aspects of their decisions on record storage.

2.2.5 Data protection act

Principle 5 of the Data Protection Act 1998 (DPA) states:

> *Personal data processed for any purpose or purposes shall not be kept*
> *for longer than is necessary for that purpose or those purposes.*

This requirement has led many organizations to assume that the legal/regulatory requirements for retention (see above) are to be taken as the actual retention period for the records concerned. In practice, however, where there is a business case for longer retention, the DPA allows this to be used.

2.2.6 Legal discovery and other retrieval purposes

When an organization is involved in litigation, there may be a requirement to produce for the court 'all the information' related to the case in progress. This process is referred to as 'discovery'.

Note

Legal discovery rules are different in Scotland compared with the rest of the United Kingdom.

Should such a position occur, the individual or organization will need to have procedures in place to identify 'all relevant information'. This may involve the searching of databases, shared drives, email systems and other document storage systems. It may also involve the restoration of information from backup media where this information is no longer available on live systems.

This process can be costly to implement unless information is well managed and retention periods are allocated and demonstrably adhered to. There are also issues such as charges of contempt of court should it subsequently be shown that all information was not provided on request.

2.3 Implementation

Now that the factors that need to be taken into account have been specified, retention periods can be identified, approved and implemented. This process may involve a large number of people within the organization and possibly some assistance from external experts.

Each retention period should be constructed as follows:

- definition of the records covered by the particular retention period;
- statement of the length of time that the records should be retained;
- reference to the relevant legal and/or regulatory condition (if applicable);
- statement of the process to be followed at the end of the retention period.

2.3.1 Record classification

The organization needs to maintain a list of the types of record that it creates and stores. There are two ways in which such a list can be developed.

- Use the record types defined in existing retention guidelines.

Example

For local government users, a group of experts has put together the Local Government Classification Scheme (LGCS). This scheme is based on a 'model' local authority and covers the records that are typically created and stored by the model authority. All functions that are potentially within the scope of 'real' local authorities are included. This scheme is intended to be used as a template for the construction of an individual local authority's classification scheme. (The LGCS includes guidelines on retention, based on legal and regulatory requirements.)

- Use locally devised record types.

These are typically devised by reviewing the activities of business units within the organization. There could be an assessment of existing paper filing systems, a review of shared drives within the IT systems and a review of email systems.

Examples of record types
- Invoices
- Statements
- Contracts
- Customer orders
- Staff human resources files
- Insurance policies

2.3.2 Functional or structural

Once a set of record types has been identified, they are best organized in a tree-like structure. There are two ways of defining the tree-like structure as follows.

- Functional

In this case, each tree 'branch' represents one of the functions of the organization, e.g. a bank might include as branches 'current accounts', 'savings accounts' and 'mortgages'.

- Structural

For this type of branch structure, each branch represents a department (or other subdivision) of the organization.

There is always an advantage in using a functional structure, as changes in internal structure do not have to be mirrored by changes in the record classification scheme.

2.3.3 Retention times

Once records have been classified, a retention period should be allocated to each record type. Retention periods should be of a fixed period of time, which is typically a number of years. The commencement date for this fixed period of time should also be specified.

The commencement time can be one of a variety of types, depending upon the record type. For example, the commencement date could be:

- creation date of the record;
- end of the current financial year;
- approval date for the next version of the record;
- at the end of the life of the individual;
- once the last item to which the record relates has been manufactured;
- once the building has been demolished and the site cleared.

These are just a few examples of events that could trigger retention periods. The trigger date may be unknown at the time of creation of the record. Thus, in order to be able to comply with unknown trigger dates, an ERMS needs to be able to interact with other corporate systems.

Example

A financial services company has decided upon a 7 year retention policy for bank accounts, to commence at the date of death of the account holder. Records such as the original application form, general correspondence and other administrative documents are held in electronic form on an ERMS. A mechanism is thus required to inform the ERMS that an individual has died, and thus to commence the fixed part of the retention period.

Along with each record type, a reference to the legal and/or regulatory condition that has been used to set the retention period should be made. Where there is a business case for extending this period, a note of the reasons should be made. Such a note may be important should there be issues with the retention periods for personal data.

It should not be assumed that retention periods, once agreed, will be fixed in time. Legislation and regulations change, so there is a need for monitoring and regular review of the retention periods. There may also be issues that arise during the conduct of business that identify the need for a longer (or shorter) retention period. Thus, retention periods should be subject to regular review.

2.3.4 Disposal

An important part of any retention policy is the details of the processes to be undertaken at the end of the retention period. Whilst in many cases, at the end of the retention period the record is immediately deleted, this may not be the case.

In some cases, the record may be of historical interest. It would thus be inappropriate for the record to be lost – in this case the record may be transferred to a record office (such as The National Archives for central government records), museum, archive or other long-term record repository.

In other cases, there may be a need to delete the record from the storage system. For digital records, this process can be fraught with problems, as there are likely to be multiple occurrences of the record. For example:

- the 'master' record is held in an ERMS system;
- there are backup copies of the records on the ERMS;
- there may be copies of the records retained from previous versions of the ERMS (such as optical disks from old systems that have been converted to Storage Area Network (SAN) storage);
- the original author may have retained copies prior to posting to the ERMS;
- individuals may have made copies of the document 'for their own use';
- there may be copies in the corporate email system, either created during the original development of the record, or by circulation of a copy of the record.

From the above list, it can be seen that, unless there is strict control over copies of a digital record, it may be impossible to identify all the occurrences of a record. This leads to issues when trying to implement a disposal policy. Having said that, a number of practical steps can be taken to ease this issue:

- there is a strict rotation of backup copies, with no long-term retention of 'old' backup media;[2]

---

[2] It should be noted that backup media is not suitable as an archiving solution. If off-line storage is required, specific archiving solutions should be used.

- storage media from old – no longer used – ERMS (or other) solutions should be destroyed once the replacement system has been fully validated;
- the process of storing a record on ERMS should include the deletion of 'local' copies;
- records stored on the ERMS should be protected from copying to local systems and to email systems;
- users should be encouraged to include links to the 'master' record rather than to attach copies of the record.

3.2 Standards bodies

In the context of this document, standards organizations responsible for defining formats that could be used for long-term preservation are listed below.

ISO	International Organization for Standardization is an international standard-setting body composed of representatives from various national standards organizations. http://www.iso.org/
BSI	BSI British Standards is the national standards body of the UK. http://www.bsigroup.com/
ITU	ITU is the United Nations agency for information and communication technologies and produces ITU Recommendations (standards). http://www.itu.int
W3C	The World Wide Web Consortium (W3C) is an international consortium where member organizations, a full-time staff and the public work together to develop web standards known as W3C Recommendations. http://www.w3.org/
IETF	The Internet Engineering Task Force (IETF) is a large, open international community of network designers, operators, vendors and researchers concerned with the evolution of the Internet's architecture. The IETF publishes protocol standards, best current practices and informational documents of various kinds. http://www.ietf.org

ECMA	ECMA International facilitates the timely creation of a wide range of global information and communications technology and consumer electronics standards. http://www.ecma-international.org/
JPEG and JBIG	JPEG and JBIG represent a wide variety of companies and academic institutions worldwide. JPEG stands for 'Joint Photographic Experts Group' and JBIG for 'Joint Bi-level Image Experts Group' – the term 'Joint' refers to the link between the standardization bodies that created these working groups, ISO and ITU. http://www.jpeg.org

3.3 Non-digital archival format

3.3.1 Paper

Open standards	BS ISO 11108:1996, *Information and documentation. Archival paper. Requirements for permanence and durability*
	The permanent paper standard, ISO 11108, introduces the concept of archival paper and unites the concepts of permanence and durability. The concepts are defined as follows: • *permanence*: the ability to remain chemically and physically stable over long periods of time;

- *durability*: the ability to resist the effects of wear and tear when in use;
- *permanent paper:* paper that during long-term storage in libraries, archives and other protected environments will undergo little or no change in properties that affect use;
- *archival paper*: paper of high permanence and high durability.

Self-containment	Yes
Embedded metadata	This is most commonly achieved by the use of 2-D or 3-D barcodes.
Document fidelity	Yes
Document interactivity	N/A
Human readable	Yes
Machine readable	Paper documents can be converted into digital documents by scanning and using Optical Character Recognition (OCR) or Barcode reading technologies.
Lifespan	Typically, manufacturers talk about a lifespan of 100+ years.
Patent and license free	Yes

3.3.2 Microfilm and microfiche

Micrographics employ processed photographic films that carry images of documents to users for transmission, storage, reading and printing. Microform images are commonly about 25 times reduced from the original document size. For special purposes, greater optical reductions such as 48 times can be used.

All microform images may be provided as positives or negatives. For use in readers and printers, negative images are preferred, that is with a dark background – the low light available to be scattered gives cleaner images.

Equipment is available for the direct writing of digital documents (typically from TIFF files) onto 16 mm microfilm or onto microfiche. Equipment is also available to scan microfilm back to the TIFF file format, for use in digital storage systems.

Open standards	BS ISO 6199, *Micrographics. Microfilming of documents on 16 mm and 35 mm silver-gelatin type microfilm. Operating procedures*
	BS ISO 6200, *Micrographics. First generation silver-gelatin microforms of source documents. Density specifications and method of measurement*
	BS 6498, *Guide to preparation of microfilm and other microforms that may be required as evidence.*
Self-containment	There is an external dependency on a suitable reader – although in an emergency, a magnifying glass and a natural light source (the sun) can be used.

Embedded metadata	As with paper, this is most commonly achieved by the use of 2-D or barcodes.
Document fidelity	Yes for bi-tonal images. Colour microfilm is also available but typically does not have the same lifespan as black and white microfilms.
Document interactivity	No
Human readable	Yes (with a magnifying aid)
Lifespan	BS 1153, *Recommendations for processing and storage of silver-gelatine-type microfilm*
	When this British Standard is complied with, silver gelatin (often the 'master' micro-film) will have a longevity of 500+ years. For typical copy microfilms, e.g. using diazo materials, storage under manufacturers' recommendations will typically achieve a lifespan of 50+ years.
Patent and license free	Yes

3.4 Digital archival formats

The formats described in this chapter can all be considered to be candidates for archival formats. Whilst the majority of the formats do not entirely meet all the criteria for an archival format, each has unique characteristics worthy of consideration.

3.4.1 ISO 19005 – PDF/A

The primary purpose of ISO 19005 is to define a file format based on PDF known as PDF/A, which provides a mechanism for representing digital documents in a manner that preserves their visual appearance over time, independent of the tools and systems used for creating, storing or rendering the files. This international standard is created as a multi-part document so that versions with greater capability can be introduced as the reference PDF specification evolves without making obsolete either systems or documents based on earlier versions.

A secondary purpose of ISO 19005 is to provide a framework for recording the context and history of digital documents in metadata within conforming files.

Another purpose of ISO 19005 is to define a framework for representing the logical structure and other semantic information of digital documents within conforming files.

These goals are accomplished by identifying the set of PDF components that may be used, and restrictions on the form of their use, within conforming PDF/A files.

3.4.1.1 ISO 19005-1

This standard defines the PDF/A format for the long-term archiving of electronic documents and is based on the PDF Reference

Version 1.4 from Adobe Systems Inc. (implemented in Adobe Acrobat 5).

The standard defines two levels of conformance – level A and level B.

Level A conformance – files adhere to the full set of requirements defined in the standard.

Level B conformance – the level B conformance requirements are intended to be those minimally necessary to ensure that the rendered visual appearance of a conforming file is preservable over the long term.

3.4.1.2 ISO 19005-2

This extends the capabilities of PDF/A described in ISO 19005-1 and is based on PDF Version 1.7 rather than PDF Version 1.4, which is used as the basis of Part 1. Many application areas will find that the capabilities available in ISO 19005-1 will adequately meet their needs and where this is the case there are no technical reasons to change. The added capabilities include:

- compliance with PDF Version 1.7 and many of the features enabled by that version;
- file attachments and PDF packages;
- transparency;
- JPEG 2000 compression;
- a new compliance level – level U.

Level U conformance requirements are similar to level B and are intended to be those necessary to ensure that not only is the rendered visual appearance of a conforming file preservable over the long term, but also any text contained in the document can be reliably extracted as a series of Unicode code points.

Open standards	BS ISO 19005-1, BS ISO 19005-2, ISO 32000 (PDF)
Self-containment	Yes (all fonts must be embedded)
Self-documenting	XMP metadata can be included within the document.
Document fidelity	Yes
Document interactivity	Limited
Human readable	No – although the XMP metadata is required to be clear text
Patent and license free	PDF reference contains a statement from Adobe Systems Inc. concerning its intellectual property and its willingness to allow perpetual, royalty-free, non-exclusive use of that property in order to promote the use of PDF. Adobe has provided ISO with a similar statement relating to XMP specification. In general, anyone may use PDF reference and XMP specification to create applications that read, write or otherwise process PDF/A files.

3.4.2 ODF (ISO/IEC 26300)

ISO/IEC 26300:2006 defines an XML schema for office applications and its semantics. The schema is suitable for office documents, including text documents, spreadsheets, charts and graphical documents like drawings or presentations but is not restricted to these kinds of document.

Open standards	ISO/IEC 26300, *Information technology. Open document format for office applications (OpenDocument) v1.0*
Self-containment	Dependent on external fonts
Self-documenting	Yes, via embedded metadata
Document fidelity	No
Document interactivity	Yes
Human readable	Yes
Patent and license free	Yes

3.4.3 Office Open XML (ISO/IEC DIS 29500[3])

Office Open XML (commonly referred to as OOXML or Open XML) is an XML-based file format specification for electronic documents such as memos, reports, books, spreadsheets, charts, presentations and word processing documents. The specification was developed by Microsoft as a successor to its binary office file formats and was handed

---

[3]At time of publication ISO/IEC 29500 is a draft International Standard.

over to ECMA International to be published as the ECMA 376 standard in December 2006.

The Office Open XML file is an Open Packaging Convention package containing the individual files that form the basis of the document. In addition to XML files with Office mark-up data, the ZIP package can also include embedded (binary) files in formats such as PNG, BMP, AVI or PDF.

An Office Open XML file may contain several documents encoded in specialized mark-up languages corresponding to applications within the Microsoft Office product line. Office Open XML defines multiple vocabularies (using 27 namespaces and 89 schema modules). The primary mark-up languages are:

- WordprocessingML – word processing;
- SpreadsheetML – spreadsheets;
- PresentationML – presentation;

For drawing:

- DrawingML;
- VML (deprecated);

Shared mark-up language materials include:

- OMML (Office Math Mark-up Language);
- extended properties;

- custom properties;
- variant types;
- custom XML data properties;
- bibliography.

In addition to the above mark-up languages, custom XML schemas can be used to extend Office Open XML.

Open standards	ECMA 376, ISO/IEC DIS 29500
Self-containment	Dependent on external fonts
Self-documenting	Yes, via embedded metadata
Document fidelity	Yes
Document interactivity	Yes
Human readable	Yes
Patent and license free	Only once the ISO/IEC standard is approved can this be confidently assumed.

3.4.4 HTML and XHTML

3.4.4.1 HTML

The HyperText Mark-up Language (HTML) is an application of the International Standard ISO 8879, *Information processing — Text and office systems — Standard Generalized Markup Language (SGML)*. It provides a simple way of structuring hypertext documents and of placing references in one document that point to another.

ISO/IEC 15445 is a refinement of the World Wide Web Consortium's (W3C's) Recommendation for HTML 4.0: it provides further rules to condition and refine the use of the W3C Recommendation in a way that emphasizes the use of stable and mature features and represents accepted SGML practice.

3.4.4.2 XHTML

XHTML is a mark-up language that has the same depth of expression as HTML but also conforms to XML syntax. Whereas HTML is an application of SGML, a very flexible mark-up language, XHTML is an application of XML, a more restrictive subset of SGML. Because they need to be well formed, true XHTML documents allow for automated processing to be performed using standard XML tools – unlike HTML, which requires a relatively complex, lenient and generally custom parser. XHTML can be thought of as the intersection of HTML and

Open standards	ISO/IEC 15445:2000(E), W3C 1999a
Self-containment	Dependent on external fonts
Self-documenting	Yes
Document fidelity	No (even with CSS and fixed positioning, there are no embedded fonts)
Document interactivity	Some interactivity via JavaScript
Human readable	Yes
Patent and license free	Yes

XML in many respects, since it is a reformulation of HTML in XML. XHTML 1.1 became a W3C recommendation on 31 May 2001.

3.4.5 SGML

SGML was originally designed to enable the sharing of machine-readable documents in large projects in government, legal and industry settings that have to remain readable for several decades. It has also been used extensively in the printing and publishing industries, but its complexity has prevented its widespread application for small-scale general-purpose use.

Open standards	ISO 8879:1986
Self-containment	Yes
Self-documenting	Yes
Document fidelity	No
Document interactivity	No
Human readable	Yes
Patent and license free	Yes

3.4.6 XML

The Extensible Mark-up Language (XML) is a general-purpose mark-up language. It is classified as an extensible language because it allows its users to define their own tags. Its primary purpose is to facilitate the sharing of structured data across different information systems, particularly via the Internet. It is used both to encode documents and serialize data.

It started as a simplified subset of SGML and is designed to be relatively human-legible. By adding semantic constraints, application languages can be implemented in XML. These include XHTML, RSS, MathML, GraphML, Scalable Vector Graphics, MusicXML and thousands of others. Moreover, XML is sometimes used as the specification language for such application languages.

XML is recommended by the World Wide Web Consortium. It is a fee-free open standard. The W3C recommendation specifies both the lexical grammar and the requirements for parsing.

Open standards	W3C recommendation
	Extensible Mark-up Language (XML) is a simple, very flexible text format derived from SGML (ISO 8879).
Self-containment	Yes
Self-documenting	Yes
Document fidelity	No
Document interactivity	No
Human readable	Yes
Patent and license free	Yes

3.4.7 MHTML

MHTML stands for MIME HTML (Multipurpose Internet Mail Extension HTML). It is a proposed standard (in 1999 and not yet approved) for including web page resources that in pages are linked externally, such as images and sound files, in the same file as the HTML code, based on RFC 2557. The included data files are encoded using MIME.

The key to MHTML is that the content is encoded as if it were an HTML email message, using the MIME type multipart/related. The first part is the HTML file, encoded normally. Subsequent parts are additional resources, identified by their original URLs.

Open standards	IETF RFC 2557 (proposal)
Self-containment	Dependent on external fonts
Self-documenting	No
Document fidelity	No
Document interactivity	No
Human readable	Partially (binary components are encoded as base-64)
Patent and license free	Yes

3.4.8 Plain text

Plain text files are usually interpreted as consisting solely of characters from a recognized character set. Well-known character sets include the ASCII character set and the Unicode character set.

There is a distinction between plain text, containing only text, new line codes and an end of file marker, and structured text, which may contain a lot of additional information, such as start and end marks of bold, italic, coloured text, start and end of paragraphs, chapter headers and numbered lists.

Open standards	ISO 14962:1997 (ASCII), ISO 10646 (Unicode/UCS)
Self-containment	Dependent on external fonts
Self-documenting	No
Document fidelity	No
Document interactivity	No
Human readable	Yes
Patent and license free	Yes

3.4.9 Image format: JPEG

JPEG (Joint Photographic Experts Group) is a lossy compression method standardized by ISO. JPEG JFIF, which is what people generally mean when they refer to 'JPEG', is a file format created by the

Independent JPEG Group (IJG) for the transport of single JPEG-compressed images.

Open standards	ISO/IEC 10918-1 (JPEG), ITU Recommendation T.81
Self-containment	Yes
Self-documenting	JPEG supports metadata sections, most commonly EXIF metadata.
	XMP packets can be embedded.
Document fidelity	Yes
Document interactivity	No
Human readable	No
Patent and license free	Yes
Image format allowable in PDF/A	Yes

3.4.10 Image format: JPEG 2000

ISO/IEC 15444, *Information technology — JPEG 2000 image coding system: Core coding system*, is a published international standard. JPEG 2000 offers both lossless and lossy compression and provides much better image quality at smaller file sizes than JPEG does.

Also published is ISO 15444-6, *Information technology — JPEG 2000 image coding system — Part 6: Compound image file format*. Part 6 deals with mixed raster content, also known as JPM format, and is aimed at compressing scanned colour documents containing both bi-tonal elements and images.

Note: The core coding system of JPEG 2000 is intended as royalty and license-fee free, not patent free.

Open standards	ISO/IEC 15444-1:2004
Self-containment	Yes
Self-documenting	JPEG 2000 supports embedding of arbitrary metadata with 'boxes'.
	XMP packets can be embedded.
Document fidelity	Yes
Document interactivity	No
Human readable	No
Patent and license free	Yes
Image format allowable in PDF/A	BS ISO 19005-1: no
	BS ISO 19005-2: yes

3.4.10.1 Related publications

PD 6777, *Guide to practical implementation of JPEG 2000*

3.4.11 Image format: JBIG2

JBIG2 is an image compression standard for bi-tonal images, developed by the Joint Bi-level Image Experts Group. It is suitable for both lossless and lossy compression. Published standards related to JBIG2 are ITU T.88:2000 and ISO/IEC 14492:2001.

The design goal for JBIG2 was to allow for lossless compression performance better than that of the existing standards and to allow for lossy compression at much higher compression ratios than the lossless ratios of the existing standards, with almost no visible degradation of quality.

Open standards	ISO/IEC 14492
Self-containment	Yes
Self-documenting	No – JBIG2 is a compression scheme, not a file format
Document fidelity	Yes
Document interactivity	No
Human readable	No
Patent and license free	Yes
Image format allowable in PDF/A	Yes

3.4.12 PNG

PNG is an extensible file format for the lossless, portable, well-compressed storage of raster images. PNG provides a patent-free replacement for the GIF file format for images, which had been subject to patent issues surrounding LZW compression.

Open standards	ISO/IEC 15948:2004
Self-containment	Yes
Self-documenting	Metadata can be embedded in iTXt chunks. XMP packets can be embedded.
Document fidelity	Yes
Document interactivity	No
Human readable	No
Patent and license free	Yes
Image format allowable in PDF/A	No

3.4.13 TIFF

TIFF format is commonly used in document imaging and document management systems. In this environment it is normally used with CCITT Group IV 2D compression, which supports black-and-white (bi-tonal) images.

Because TIFF format supports multiple pages, multi-page documents can be saved as single TIFF files rather than as a series of files for each scanned page.

TIFF files are capable of including images that use a range of compression schemes including Group 3 (ITU-T Recommendation T.3), Group 4 (ITU-T Recommendation T.563), RLE, LZW, JPEG, Packbits and others.

The final revision of the TIFF Format (Version 6.0, published in 1992) had a number of flaws, most notably with respect to the support for JPEG images. Whilst supplements have been issued to clarify matters, software implementations vary significantly hence it is not recommended to adopt TIFF for long-term preservation of files that include JPEG images.

Open standards	ISO 12369:2004
Self-containment	Yes
Self-documenting	TIFF supports standard and custom tags that can be used to store metadata. A custom tag has been defined to allow embedding of XMP metadata.
Document fidelity	Yes
Document interactivity	No
Human readable	No
Patent and license free	Yes
Image format allowable in PDF/A	TIFF itself is a file format not an image format.
	Both Group 3 and Group 4 image formats, commonly used in TIFF files for bi-tonal scanned documents, are supported in PDF/A.

3.4.14 SVG

Scalable Vector Graphics (SVG) is an XML-based graphics language that describes images with vector shapes, text and embedded raster graphics. Originally developed by Adobe, SVG 1.1 is a W3C 2003 recommendation. The format should be considered as an option for archiving of drawing and CAD files.

Open standards	SVG 1.1 is a W3C 2003 recommendation.
Self-containment	Dependent on external fonts
Self-documenting	Yes. As SVG is an XML format, XMP or other XML metadata can be embedded.
Document fidelity	Yes
Document interactivity	Yes
Human readable	Yes
Patent and license free	Yes

3.4.15 Video and audio formats

The Moving Picture Experts Group, commonly referred to as simply MPEG, is a working group of ISO/IEC charged with the development of video and audio encoding standards. MPEG's official designation is ISO/IEC JTC1/SC29 WG11.

MPEG has standardized the following compression formats and ancillary standards.

MPEG-1: initial video and audio compression standard. Later used as the standard for Video CD and includes the popular Layer 3 (MP3) audio compression format.

MPEG-2: transport, video and audio standards for broadcast-quality television. Used for over-the-air digital television ATSC, DVB and ISDB, digital satellite TV services like Dish Network, digital cable television signals, SVCD and with slight modifications as the VOB (Video OBject) files that carry the images on DVDs.

MPEG-4: expands MPEG-1 to support video/audio 'objects', 3D content, low bit-rate encoding and support for digital rights management. Several new, higher efficiency video standards are incorporated including MPEG-4 Part 10 (or Advanced Video Coding or H.264). MPEG-4 Part 10 may be used on HD DVD and Blu-ray discs, along with VC-1 and MPEG-2.

Open standards	ISO/IEC 11172, ISO/IEC 13818, ISO/IEC 14496
Self-containment	Yes
Self-documenting	Yes (MPEG-7)
Document fidelity	Yes
Document interactivity	N/A
Human readable	No
Patent and license free	MPEG-4 is patented proprietary technology. This means that, although the software to create and play back MPEG-4 videos may be readily available, a license is needed to use it legally in countries that acknowledge software patents. Patents covering MPEG-4 are claimed by over two dozen companies. The MPEG Licensing Authority (see http://www.mpegla.com) licenses patents.

MPEG-7: a formal XML-based metadata system for describing the content of MPEG files.

MPEG-21: defines an XML-based 'Rights Expression Language' standard as a means of sharing digital rights/permissions/restrictions for digital content.

3.4.16 XPS

The XML Paper Specification (XPS) describes the format of a general-purpose document made available by Microsoft to facilitate the easy exchange of documents between applications, platforms and

Open standards	XPS is a planned ECMA standard that will provide a formal standard for an XML-based electronic paper format and XML-based page description language that is consistent with existing implementations of the format called the XML Paper Specification (XPS) created by Microsoft
Self-containment	Yes (fonts can be embedded in XPS)
Self-documenting	Yes
Document fidelity	Yes
Document interactivity	No
Human readable	Yes (once decompressed, except for image elements)
Patent and license free	This cannot be assured until XPS reaches the level of an ISO standard

hardware systems. XPS documents offer a convenient alternative to paper documents for viewing, printing, transferring and archiving.

3.5 Guidance for specific document categories

Table 3.1 can be used as an initial guide to the mapping of source format to document format. An organization's requirements will further refine the choice of formats as needs are matched to the characteristics of the formats.

3.5.1 Source format to archive format mapping

Table 3.1: Guide to the mapping of source format to document format

Source format	Archive format										
	TEXT	PDF/A	XML	ODF	OOXML	JPEG	JPEG2000	JBIG2	TIFF	SVG	MPEG
Unstructured text	✓	✓	✓								
Structured text		✓	✓	✓	✓				✓		
Office documents		✓		✓	✓				✓		
Presentation graphics		✓		✓	✓						
Image		✓				✓	✓	✓	✓		
Audio											✓
Video											✓
Vector graphics/CAD										✓	
Others		✓									

3.5.2 Archiving emails

Emails with attachments present a particular challenge as they are in effect compound documents. There are essentially two alternatives for dealing with this issue as follows.

3.5.2.1 Separation

In this approach, the email is decomposed into its components, i.e. message and attachments, and each component is then archived. Each attachment needs to be converted to an archival format.

3.5.2.2 Embedding

This approach involves creating a single archive file with the message and embedded attachments. PDF/A-2 can be used for this purpose as it allows file attachments. Each attachment must itself be PDF/A compliant. Another possible solution is MHTML.

3.5.3 Archiving web pages and sites

Web pages typically reference a set of resources that may include images, sound and video. In addition, websites include interactive elements ranging from simple intra-site hyperlinks to complex interaction with back end systems – the latter cannot easily be preserved.

In a similar fashion to the long-term preservation of emails, there are two approaches as follows.

3.5.3.1 Separation

In this approach, the website is decomposed into its static components, i.e. HTML, images, PDF files etc., and each component is then converted to an archival format.

3.5.3.2 Embedding

This approach involves creating a single archive file with the web page or website and embedded resources. MHTML was in part designed for this purpose and could be considered.

PDF/A-2 can also be used for this purpose as it allows file attachments and also supports hyperlinks. Each attachment must itself be PDF/A compliant.

Storage media

4

As noted previously, there are two major issues with long-term preservation of digital records – the choice of storage format and storage media. This chapter looks at the various options that exist for the long-term physical storage of digital records. As a comparison, issues with the long-term storage of paper and microfilm-based records are also included. This chapter describes the options and weighs up the benefits of each.

Organizations need to keep records of their activities and facilities to comply with legal requirements and to fulfil obligations to the relevant regulators and government bodies. There may be particular obligations written into operational licences that require certain records to be retained for a long period of time.

Historically, prior to electronic storage all records were retained on paper, or in some cases on microfilm. However, with modern electronic systems, records are now being retained in digital form. This chapter examines a number of long-term storage methods, using both physical and electronic media. It compares the merits and issues of each method, to enable an informed decision to be made in a particular situation.

In addition, for each storage media there are recommendations on the methods to be used for the destruction of stored records. Whilst with some media types, destruction is easy, for others it is in practice very difficult to destroy individual records.

The storage media that are discussed in this chapter are as follows:

- paper;
- microfilm;
- magnetic tape, reel and cartridge;
- optical disk;
- electronic on-line systems.

Each of these storage medium types is reviewed, and the various advantages and disadvantages are discussed. Each is reviewed for longevity, and hence their suitability for the long-term storage of digital records.

4.1 Paper

4.1.1 General

Paper has been used to store information for thousands of years. It is legally admissible, has a high evidential value and is robust. It can be read without the aid of technology. However, it is bulky and thus costly to store. It is also costly to produce backup copies and store them separately. There are also long-term issues with paper storage, which needs environmental conditioning in storage areas.

Where the preservation strategy includes the retention of documents in paper form for longer than about 50 years, it is recommended that archival quality paper is used.

4.1.2 Risks

There are a number of risks associated with storage on paper. These risks can be divided into the following categories.

4.1.2.1 Only one copy

Because paper is bulky and time consuming to copy, the tendency is for only one copy to be held. This leads to significant levels of risk, either due to the potential disasters in the storage areas or due to the loss of a document due to mis-filing.

4.1.2.2 Multiple copies

Where multiple copies may be held, there can be issues relating to the designation of 'the master' and to version control. This is typically managed by the strict adherence to records management policies and procedures.

4.1.2.3 Alteration of documents

It is a relatively simple process to alter a paper document, particularly where an electronic copy exists. High levels of security are required to protect vital paper documents from alteration.

4.1.2.4 Poor storage conditions

Paper documents are prone to fading and physical degradation over time. The longevity of paper documents in storage is directly related to their storage conditions. Where paper documents are stored for a long period of time, the recommendations of BS 5454:2000, *Recommendations for the storage and exhibition of archival documents*, should be met. This has cost implications, particularly where large volumes of paper documents are stored.

4.1.2.5 Electronic readability

Many documents are created and maintained electronically. When printed on paper, readability on electronic systems is compromised. Whilst electronic documents can be re-inputted, either manually or by the use of optical character recognition technology, neither method is error free.

There are also some types of electronic document that lose significant amounts of information once printed, e.g. where the original electronic file is in three dimensions.

4.1.2.6 Loss of metadata

When an electronic document is printed, a potentially significant amount of metadata may be lost. For example, when an email is printed, the information related to the routing of the email from sender to recipient can be lost.

4.1.3 Applications

Paper storage systems are most appropriate for an organization's high value original vital documents. Original contracts and drawings of plant and equipment are possible examples in this category. It may also be appropriate to retain the original of documents that will have historical value in the future. Another category of document where a paper original will be required to be retained is where legislation and/or regulation require them to be stored. Instances in this last category are becoming rarer as electronic storage is perceived to be an acceptable storage mechanism.

4.1.4 Destruction

The destruction of paper records is generally straightforward. The method implemented (and there may be an advantage in using multiple methods) needs to be chosen on the basis of the risk of non-destruction taking place.

The following are methods of destroying paper records:

- place in the general waste (little security, inexpensive);
- separate records from the general waste and subject them to a confidential waste process consisting of separate collection points in offices (secure, can be costly);
- install document shredders on-site (can be office based or central);
- use an external, confidential waste contractor, using either shredding or incineration.

4.2 Microfilm

4.2.1 General

Microfilm has been used for over 100 years to store images of paper documents and more recently to store images of electronic documents. It has been used for the storage of legally sensitive documents for many years. Such systems, when well managed, can be used to replace the need to store original documents. Microfilm is costly to produce but inexpensive to store because of its small size. It is also inexpensive to produce microfilm copies for off-site storage. The only requirement for readability is a magnifying system, perhaps by the use of microfilm readers. It is also inexpensive to create paper copies for future use.

4.2.2 Risks

Once committed to microfilm, documents are protected from alteration or degeneration. However, there are other risks to be taken into account as follows.

4.2.2.1 Microfilm degradation

It is important that microfilm is produced to the appropriate British Standard – BS ISO 6199:2005 and BS 1153:1992. Improper production and, in particular, improper processing and storage, can result in reduced storage life.

4.2.2.2 Evidential value

Where an original document is no longer available, an image held on microfilm may be challenged for authenticity. It is then necessary to demonstrate that the image is a true copy of the original document. This is best achieved by following the recommendations of BS 6498. This standard contains procedures to be followed when making microfilms that may be needed as evidence.

4.2.2.3 Electronic readability

Like paper, microfilm is an image form of an original document. It cannot directly be read into a computer system for further use. Again, re-inputting or optical character recognition techniques will be needed in this case.

4.2.3 Applications

Many organizations now perceive microfilm as old technology that should no longer be used. However, where documents (either paper or electronic) need to be stored for a long period of time (say >10 years), and are likely never to be accessed during their storage life, then microfilm is still a viable medium.

Microfilm has a proven longevity (assuming correct processing and storage), is inexpensive to copy and does not suffer from technology obsolescence. Thus, for any records that need to be retained, e.g. to be used in the event of an accident or disaster, but are not needed for everyday use, microfilm may well be the best storage option.

A current example of where microfilm storage is being used is with the 2001 census. All the census forms were scanned, and the resultant TIFF electronic images were used for data acquisition and analysis. For long-term storage, these TIFF images were written to microfilm. When the census data are published in 2101, it is planned to scan the microfilm with the then-current equipment.

4.2.4 Destruction

Microfilm records can only be destroyed economically on a per-unit basis – as a complete roll of film, a single microfiche or a single frame of jacketed/aperture card mounted film. This factor is important and should be taken into consideration when deciding on the content of a unit of microfilm – they should all have the same retention period.

Microfilm can be destroyed by any of the following methods:

- shredding – but use a small cut shredder as paper shredders can leave film clips from which information can be read;
- chemical – chemicals can be obtained that dissolve the emulsion of a microfilm, thus destroying the records (a messy process);
- incineration.

4.3 Magnetic tape

4.3.1 General

Magnetic tape technology has been used for over 50 years for the storage of computer data. It has progressed from the ½ inch reel to reel tape systems to modern cartridge based systems. Such systems are frequently used for computer backup systems as the media used are inexpensive and reusable. Data transfer rates can be very high. Multiple copies can be written or tapes can be duplicated to produce backup copies. However, as a long-term storage medium there are doubts about longevity. Technology (typically the original computer system) is needed to read the tapes.

4.3.2 Risks

Documents written to magnetic tape will be in a form that is recoverable by computer systems. Risks involved in magnetic tape storage are as follows.

4.3.2.1 Loss of readability

There have been a number of recent cases where data stored on magnetic tape can no longer be read by a computer system. Owing to the nature of the medium, the magnetic fields within the medium will change with time. Whilst modern cartridge systems suffer less from the problem, the old reel tape systems had a maximum recommended storage life of 1 year. Modern tape silo systems use spare capacity to check the readability of stored data, copying it to newer media whenever necessary.

4.3.2.2 Physical damage

As magnetic tape needs to be moved past read/write heads during reading and writing operations, there is potential for physical damage. Such damage, e.g. to the edges of the tape, may cause readability issues. Duplicates will need to be stored to reduce this risk.

4.3.2.3 Technology obsolescence

Technology issues can result from hardware and/or software obsolescence. Over time, equipment to read magnetic tape will become out of date and thus unsupported by the manufacturers. This requires a repeated migration onto newer storage technology from time to time.

Computer software also moves forward, and backward compatibility is not always guaranteed. It may thus be necessary for data to be converted from one software system to another from time to time.

4.3.3 Applications

Magnetic tape storage systems for document archiving are becoming rarer, being replaced mainly by on-line storage systems. However, they are widely used for backup and short-term storage systems. These systems may be suitable, where the technology already exists in an organization for the short-term (say <7 years) storage of information. Thus, they may be appropriate for financial records and other administration-type applications.

4.3.4 Destruction

As was the case with microfilm, it is only possible to destroy magnetic media on a per-item basis. However, it might be practical to destroy individual records on a magnetic tape by copying all the records that need to be retained to another magnetic tape and then destroying the original magnetic tape.

Destruction can be achieved by:

- overwriting with new data (proceed with care – there are forensic techniques that may be able to recover previous recordings, and also does the new data overwrite all of the data?);

- degaussing – by re-magnetizing the tape;
- physical destruction by shredding/incineration.

4.4 Optical disk

4.4.1 General

When optical disk was first made available for corporate data storage, it was seen as a good long-term storage medium. However, the technological progress of optical media, as well as other storage media, has led to difficulties in long-term storage applications. There are many types of optical medium to choose from. A number of the older optical systems have become obsolete, causing readability issues. Whilst storage media are inexpensive, data transfer rates can be slow. There are also issues with the long-term stability of some brands of optical disk.

There are three major classes of optical disk:

- non-rewritable Write Once Read Many (WORM);
- non-rewritable erasable;
- rewritable.

Records written to optical disks of the non-rewritable WORM type can only be deleted by the total destruction of the disk. Erasable disks cannot be reused. Rewritable disks can be reused (usually a limited number of times).

4.4.2 Risks

Optical disk technology suffers from two major problems when used for long-term storage of information as follows.

4.4.2.1 Technology obsolescence

Like magnetic tape, optical technology moves forward, and new media types and larger storage capacities are made available. The original optical disk technology (now around 10+ years old) is no longer available. One example where this has caused a problem is in the original scanning of the Doomsday book. The images were stored on optical disk, which became obsolescent. Old technology that was still operational had to be found to retrieve the stored images.

There is a current gradual migration away from CD systems to DVD systems for small volume optical storage. Similarly, high volume optical technology is slowly increasing in capacity.

4.4.2.2 Media life

A recent study in the USA[4] has demonstrated that it is important to use high quality CD media if reliable long-term storage is required.

---

[4] http://www.itl.nist.gov/iad/894.05/docs/StabilityStudy.pdf

This report was published by the US Government Information Preservation Working Group (GIPWG). They concluded that 'initial results show that high quality optical media have very stable characteristics and may be suitable for long-term storage applications. However, results also indicate that significant differences exist in the stability of recordable optical media from different manufacturers.'

4.4.3 Applications

A few years ago, optical disk was the primary medium for long-term storage of electronic information. For typical storage technologies, their storage capacities and costs, see Table 4.1.

Where multiple optical disks are required, a range of jukeboxes are available to automate medium change requests. Where such systems are used, access to any particular stored document is typically <10 seconds, dependent upon jukebox activity levels.

Table 4.1 gives a comparison of optical media types.

Thus, optical disk systems are useful for the storage of all types of electronic document. Where storage life of >5 years is involved, the cost of medium migration will need to be added to media and system costs.

Table 4.1: *Typical storage technologies, their storage capacities and costs*

Medium	Description	Capacity per disk	Media cost per TB[a]
CD-R	CD-Rom	650 MB	£770
DVD-R	Digital Versatile Disk Recordable	4.7 GB	£212
WORM	Write Once Read Many	9.1 GB	£6,050
UDO	Ultra Density Optical	23 GB	£924
PDD	Professional Disk for Data	30 GB	£1,320
SDLT[b]	Super Digital Linear Tape	300 GB	£220

[a] At typical current prices

[b] Included for comparison purposes

4.4.4 Destruction

Like magnetic tape, non-rewritable WORM type optical disks can only be destroyed on a per-unit basis. Records stored on erasable and rewritable disks can be erased or overwritten. Again, care should be taken when reusing optical disks, as there are forensic techniques that may enable the reconstruction of overwritten records.

4.5 On-line storage

4.5.1 General

Electronic on-line storage systems are developing at a rapid rate. Fault tolerant systems are now available giving high reliability and fast access. Whilst the initial capital outlay can be high, ongoing costs can be low. The use of mirrored systems can result in little need for backup to removable media, with the associated resource and storage costs. These systems can provide some security against technological advances by enabling new technology to be seamlessly introduced without affecting stored data.

4.5.2 Risks

In many ways, the use of modern on-line storage systems results in the least risk to stored data. Examples of such technologies include magnetic tape libraries, optical disk jukeboxes, RAID array systems and the newer secure storage systems such as the EMC Centera system.[5] As well as the software redundancy issues discussed below, the main risk for on-line storage systems is the high initial cost. Most, if not all of these technologies are driven from corporate IT systems. By their very nature, they have a high initial capital cost, plus an ongoing maintenance cost. Where high availability mirrored systems are used, routine procedures such as backup procedures may no longer be necessary, resulting in reduced operational costs.

4.5.3 Applications

On-line storage systems are most appropriate where 'instant' access is required to stored information. Thus, a typical application would be in

---

[5] http://www.emc.com/products/systems/centera.jsp?openfolder=platform

call centres or line-of-business applications where access to customer information is needed quickly.

4.5.4 Destruction

Records written to magnetic disk systems (such as those used in SAN/ RAID/server systems) can be individually deleted and overwritten. There are also software/hardware combinations that configure a magnetic disk to operate in a WORM mode (see 4.4), thus protecting stored records.

As with most electronic record storage systems, care is needed when deleting individual or groups of records. It is well known that a simple 'delete' operation does not remove the record from the system – recovery is often a user option, e.g. from the recycle bin. A more permanent deletion can be performed by deleting the 'deleted' records from the recycle bin.

However, again there are forensic techniques that can be used to recover deleted records (assuming of course that the records have also been deleted from backup media) should this be necessary. There are some software systems that overwrite 'deleted' records with a 'noise' recording a number of times, thus reducing the possibility of record recovery.

4.6 Summary

Table 4.2 gives the recommended options for long-term storage of records.

Table 4.2: Recommended options for long-term storage of records

Medium	Usage
Paper	Long-term storage of high value, vital business records
Microfilm	Long-term storage of rarely accessed records
Magnetic tape	Short-term storage of backup data
Optical disk	Medium-term storage of occasion-ally accessed records – long-term storage where regular medium migration is anticipated
On-line	Medium-term storage where imme-diate access is required

Metadata 5

5.1 Metadata in long-term preservation of digital documents

Documenting archived records has always been a feature of archives, which use various types of catalogue system to capture information on large volumes of records.

It is critical that document metadata is preserved alongside the document itself. In many modern systems, metadata is stored in a database that references the document.

Key point

An XML-based approach is recommended as a method for recording metadata. This approach is widely adopted, and the XML format itself meets the key requirements for long-term preservation.

Furthermore, there are a number of standard XML-based metadata schemas that can be readily used as a solution or basis for the recording of document metadata.

For long-term preservation, the metadata must be stored either in the document itself (using the XMP model for PDF/A) or as a separate external file, possibly as part of an encapsulated archive file.

Each document class has one or more XML schemas associated with it. The schemas may be one of a number of standard schemas such as Dublin Core or custom extension schemas. In addition, file provenance and history information must be recorded using either XMP or equivalent.

5.2 The purpose of metadata

Key point

In long-term preservation, metadata is the information necessary for adequate preservation of the archived documents. They can be categorized as provenance, reference, fixity and context information, as described in Chapter 6.

In long-term preservation, the purpose of metadata can be described as follows:

- to facilitate the retrieval of documents;
- to provide additional contextual information about the document;
- to provide details of the provenance of the file for legal and other reasons;
- to provide technical details of the file format used.

5.3 Metadata formats

5.3.1 XML

Extensible Mark-up Language (XML) is W3C recommended and is a simple, flexible text format derived from SGML (ISO 8879). Originally designed to meet the challenges of large-scale electronic publishing, XML also plays an increasingly important role in the exchange of a wide variety of data on the Web and is ideal as a metadata storage format.

5.3.2 RDF

RDF (Resource Description Framework) is a W3C standard XML framework for describing and interchanging metadata. The simple format of resources, properties and statements allows RDF to describe robust metadata, such as ontological structures. As opposed to topic maps, RDF is more decentralized because the XML is usually stored along with the resources.

5.3.3 XMP

XMP (Extensible Metadata Platform) facilitates embedding metadata in files using a subset of RDF. Most notably, XMP supports embedding metadata in PDF and many image formats, though it is designed to support nearly any file type.

5.3.4 ISO Topic Maps (ISO/IEC 13250)

This is a standard for describing knowledge structures and associating them with information resources. The topics, associations and occurrences that comprise topic maps allow them to describe complex structures such as ontologies. They are usually implemented using XML (XML Topic Maps, or XTM). As opposed to RDF, topic maps are more centralized because all information is contained in the map rather than associated with the resources.

5.4 Metadata schemas

5.4.1 Standard schemas

5.4.1.1 Dublin Core (ISO 15836:2003)

The Dublin Core Metadata Element Set is a vocabulary of fifteen properties for use in resource description. The name 'Dublin' results from its origin at a 1995 invitational workshop in Dublin, Ohio; 'core' is included because its elements are broad and generic, usable for describing a wide range of resources.

5.4.1.2 XMP schemas

A number of pre-defined XMP schemas have been defined by Adobe in the XMP specification. The XMP Media Management Schema, designed primarily for use by digital asset management systems, has some value for long-term archiving. A number of the properties are recommended for use in the PDA/A standard.

5.4.1.3 eGIF: UK Government standard schemas

eGIF is a set of policies and standards to enable information to flow seamlessly across the public sector, providing citizens and businesses with better access to public services.

The e-Government Metadata Standard (e-GMS) lays down the elements, refinements and encoding schemas to be used by government officers when creating metadata for their information resources or when designing search systems for information systems. The e-GMS forms part of the e-GIF.

5.4.1.4 Specialized and industry-specific standard schemas

A good many industry bodies work towards defining specialized XML schemas that can be reused by organizations. A number of common examples are:

- Open Applications Group's Integration Specification (OAGIS);
- PISCES XML – commercial property, Home Information Packs (HIP);
- OASIS Universal Business Language (UBL);

- ACORD – insurance industry;
- MISMO – mortgage industry;
- XBRL – business reporting;
- HR-XML – human resources;
- HL7 – health profession.

5.5 Custom schemas

In many cases, standard schemas may only provide a starting point for the schema needed to meet the requirements listed in 5.2. In such cases, a custom schema needs to be designed and documented. XML Schema is the preferred method for formally defining schemas.

5.6 Data standards

In order to avoid ambiguity and ensure correct future interpretation of metadata, standards for the format of attribute data should be defined and followed. Where available, pre-defined data standards should be selected.

5.6.1 ISO standards

BSI/ISO standards define a wide range of data standards, such as:

- ISO 8601 – date and time formats;
- ISO 3166 – country codes;

- ISO 4217 – currency codes;
- ISO 639 – languages;
- ISO 10383 – codes for exchanges and markets.

5.7 UK Government

The Government Data Standards Catalogue sets out the rationale, approach and rules for setting and agreeing the set of Government Data Standards (GDS) to be used in the schemas.

5.8 Metadata location

Many of the file formats discussed in 5.3 have the ability to embed metadata within the file itself. Examples are the embedding of XMP metadata within a PDF/A compliant file, or storing metadata within <META> HTML tags.

Benefits of embedded metadata are:

- no risk of separation of document and data;
- the document and metadata cannot be independently updated;
- a document viewer will typically be able to display the embedded metadata.

Benefits of external metadata are:

- always human readable;
- it can apply to all file types;
- it is possible to update the metadata without updating the document;
- metadata can be read without special knowledge of file formats.

5.9 Technical metadata

There is a need to record technical details of the archived files including details such as:

- format;
- version;
- producer;
- file size;
- checksum.

5.10 Other relevant standards

ISO/IEC 11179, *Information technology — Metadata registries (MDR)*.

ISO 23081-1, *Information and documentation — Records management processes — Metadata for records — Part 1: Principles*.

Archive creation and maintenance 6

A recommended overall model for the creation and maintenance of archives is provided by the OAIS model, which is published as ISO 14721:2003, *Space data and information transfer systems — Open archival information system — Reference model.*

> **Key point**
> The OAIS model defines the foundation, concepts and functions required of any archival system, without being prescriptive about the technical implementation.

6.1 Core concepts

The OAIS model is based around a number of key concepts, the most important of which are detailed below.

6.1.1 Information package

This is the content information and associated preservation description information that is needed to aid in the preservation of the content information. The information package has associated packaging information used to delimit and identify the content information and preservation description information.

6.1.2 Submission information package (SIP)

An information package that is delivered by the producer to the OAIS for use in the construction of one or more AIPs.

6.1.3 Archival information package (AIP)

An information package, consisting of the content information and the associated preservation description information (PDI), which is preserved within an OAIS.

6.1.3.1 AIP package design

The AIP consists of three components: metadata, data and packaging. Each component consists of one or more files. The metadata component will typically consist of XML schemas containing information describing the archival object. The data component consists of all the data files (bitstreams) that comprise the archival object. There may be multiple versions of the data file, each in a different format. The packaging component encapsulates the metadata and data components, creating a single entity or 'self-extracting archive' that is the AIP.

6.1.4 Preservation description information (PDI)

The PDI is the information that is necessary for adequate preservation of the content information and can be categorized as provenance, reference, fixity and context information.

6.1.4.1 Provenance information

> **Definition: provenace information**
> The information that documents the history of the content information.

This includes details of:

- the origin or source of the content information;
- any changes that may have taken place since it was originated;
- who has had custody of it since it was originated.

Examples of provenance information are the principal investigator who recorded the data and the information concerning its storage, handling and conversions/migrations.

6.1.4.2 Reference information

> **Definition: reference information**
> The information that documents the mechanisms used to provide assigned identifiers for the content information.

The reference information also provides identifiers that allow outside systems to refer, unambiguously, to a particular content information.

An example of reference information is an ISBN.

6.1.4.3 Context information

Definition: context information

The information that documents the relationship of the content information to its environment.

This information includes:

- why the content information was created;
- how it relates to other content information objects.

6.1.4.4 Fixity information

Definition: fixity information

The information that documents the authentication mechanisms and provides authentication keys to ensure that the content information object has not been altered in an undocumented manner.

An example is a cyclical redundancy check (CRC) code for a file.

6.1.5 Dissemination information package (DIP)

Definition: dissemination information package

The information package, derived from one or more AIPs, received by the consumer in response to a request to the OAIS.

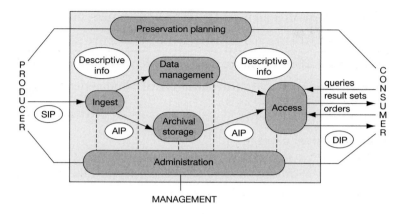

Figure 6.1: *Core functions provided by an OAIS*

6.2 OAIS functional model

The core functions provided by an OAIS are shown in Figure 6.1.

6.2.1 Producer

These are the system(s) that provide the objects to be preserved, along with relevant metadata. The producer is responsible for generating SIPs for submission to the ingest process. Often this will be the back end of the archive function in a records management system.

6.2.2 Ingest

This is the OAIS process that contains the services and functions that accept submission information packages from producers, prepares archival information packages for storage, and ensures that archival information packages and their supporting descriptive information become established within the OAIS. The process is also responsible for validation of the authenticity and format of the submitted package.

6.2.3 Archival storage

This is the OAIS process that contains the services and functions used for the storage and retrieval of archival information packages. This includes functions to migrate AIPs from one physical device to another.

6.2.4 Data management

This is the OAIS entity that contains the services and functions for populating, maintaining and accessing a wide variety of information. Some examples of this information are catalogues and inventories on what may be retrieved from archival storage, processing algorithms that may be run on retrieved data, consumer access statistics, consumer billing, event based orders, security controls and OAIS schedules, policies and procedures.

6.2.5 Access

This entity provides the services and functions that support consumers in determining the existence, description, location and availability of information stored in the OAIS, and allows consumers to request and receive information products. Access functions include communicating with consumers to receive requests, applying controls to limit access to specially protected information, coordinating the execution of requests to successful completion, generating responses (dissemination information packages, result sets, reports) and delivering the responses to consumers.

6.2.6 Administration

This entity provides the services and functions for the overall operation of the archive system. Administration functions include soliciting and negotiating submission agreements with producers, auditing submissions to ensure that they meet archive standards and maintaining configuration management of system hardware and software. It also provides functions for disposing of AIPs and updating AIPs to include conversions to newer standard file formats.

6.2.7 Preservation planning

This entity provides the services and functions for monitoring the environment of the OAIS and providing recommendations to ensure that the information stored in the OAIS remains accessible to the designated user community over the long term, even if the original computing environment becomes obsolete. Preservation planning functions include evaluating the contents of the archive and periodically recommending archival information updates to convert or migrate current archive holdings, developing recommendations for archive standards and policies and monitoring changes in the technology environment and in the designated community's service requirements and knowledge base. Preservation planning also designs IP templates and provides design assistance and review to specialize these templates into SIPs and AIPs for specific submissions. Preservation planning also develops detailed conversion and migration plans, software prototypes and test plans to enable implementation of administration conversion and migration goals.

Related standards and publications

7

This chapter looks at a number of BSI and ISO publications related to the preservation of electronic records. This field is expanding rapidly, and additional information is being published on a regular basis by a number of different committees.

7.1 The OAIS model

The reference model for an open archival information system (OAIS) was originally developed by the Consultative Committee for Space Data Systems. It is 'for use in developing a broader consensus on what is required for an archive to provide permanent, or indefinite long-term, preservation of digital information.'

The OAIS model is published as ISO 14721:2003, *Space data and information transfer systems — Open archival information system — Reference model.*

An additional publication related to the model is ISO 20652:2006, *Space data and information transfer systems — Producer-archive interface — Methodology abstract standard.*

7.1.1 Preservation systems

The OAIS model includes a section on digital preservation – which it notes requires the preservation of the digital information and the preservation of access to the digital information.

Two issues are dealt with by the model. Firstly, the preservation of digital information as it is migrated across media and converted across formats, and secondly the preservation of access services to digital information as technology changes and software is ported to new systems, wrapped to maintain consistent interfaces or emulated to support legacy applications.

The model notes that, owing to the development of new technologies, and the rapid obsolescence of old systems, digital information will need to be moved across systems on a regular basis. The model notes four approaches to digital preservation:

- refreshment – where digital information is copied from one storage medium to another, keeping the structures and hardware types consistent;
- replication – where digital information is copied to a new type of storage medium, without changes to the underlying formats;
- repackaging – where the format of the digital information is modified in a minor way to be acceptable to replacement software systems;
- transformation – where digital information undergoes major structural changes to enable preservation and access by new systems.

In all cases, there is a requirement to preserve the information content of the digital record.

7.1.2 Methodology

The methodology for long-term preservation as defined within the OAIS model centres around a well-defined process, creating an archival packet for each document that includes the original digital document, XML metadata and the archival format equivalent. As time progresses, the choice of archive formats may expand and new formats may be more appropriate for use, hence the archival packet may be extended with additional archive files converted from the earlier files. No files are ever removed from the archive packet. Audit trails sufficient to establish the provenance of each file are required.

7.2 Records management

The ISO Records Management Committee (ISO/TC 46/SC 11) is currently (at the time of publication) working on the drafting of ISO/TR 26102, *Records management — Requirements for the long-term preservation of electronic records*. This ISO Technical Report provides a framework for the preservation of electronic records within which organizations can operate. The publication is not prescriptive as to the nature of information being preserved.

7.3 Document management

The ISO Document Management Applications Committee (ISO TC 171) has published ISO/TR 18492:2005, *Long-term preservation of electronic document-based information.*

This Technical Report provides practical methodological guidance for the long-term preservation and retrieval of authentic electronic document-based information, when the retention period exceeds the expected life of the technology (hardware and software) used to create and maintain the information.

It takes into account the role of technology-neutral information technology standards in supporting long-term access.

7.3.1 Content

This publication notes that an information preservation strategy should include:

- media renewal;
- metadata management;
- conversion and migration strategies;
- conversion and migration policy;
- security management.

7.4 Legal admissibility

Where there is a requirement to retain electronic records as evidence, potentially for use in the adversarial environment of the courtroom, it is important to ensure that the records are legally admissible and that they carry the maximum possible weight of evidence.

BIP 0008-1:2004, *Code of practice for legal admissibility and evidential weight of information stored electronically*, deals with these issues.

7.4.1 Content

BIP 0008-1 includes five elements:

- information management policy;
- duty of care, including information security and consultations;
- procedures and processes;
- enabling technology;
- audit trails.

7.5 PDF/A

ISO 19005-1 defines a record preservation format based on the well-known PDF format. The objective of the format is to enable, on any computer platform (current or in the future), a record to be displayed in exactly the same layout/structure as when it was originally stored.

In order to achieve this objective, two elements are included within the standard:

- the storage format is fully defined;
- all the resources necessary to display the record are included within the file content.

References

8

1   ISO 14721:2003, *Space data and information transfer systems — Open archival information system — Reference model.*

2   ISO 15836:2003, *Information and documentation — The Dublin Core metadata element set.*
    http://www.niso.org/international/SC4/n515.pdf

3   ISO 19005, *Document management — Electronic document file format for long-term preservation.*

4   ISO/IEC 26300, *Information technology. Open document format for office applications (OpenDocument) v1.0.*

5   ISO/IEC DIS 29500 (ECMA-376), *Information technology — Office Open XML file formats.*

6   ISO TR/18492, *Long-term preservation of electronic document-based information.*

7   BIP 0008-1:2004, *Code of practice for legal admissibility and evidential weight of information stored electronically.*

Annex A – Policy document

This annex contains an example of a policy document for digital preservation (see 1.7). It can be used as a template for the development of a policy for a specific organization, or for a particular department/process within an organization.

The policy should be developed in conjunction with the business unit(s) involved, with representatives of the IT and other departments as necessary. When completed, it should be approved and signed-off by the senior management group within the organization.

XYZ Limited

ABC System

Policy document for digital preservation (from BIP 0089:2008)

Contents

1. Scope

2. Information covered

3. Preservation requirements

4. Document retention

5. Archive model

6. Storage media

7. File formats

8. Metadata standards

9. Responsibilities

10. Preservation planning

Approved by (signature):		
Name:		
Position:		
Date:		

1. Scope

This document is the digital preservation policy for XYZ Limited. It is part of the company's information strategy.

This policy is applicable to all business units within XYZ Limited and its associated companies.

2. Information covered

This policy applies to all information stored in an electronic form, where the retention period in accordance with the XYZ Limited Retention Policy is greater than 8 years[6] from the date of storage.

3. Preservation requirements

This clause of the policy specifies the requirements for digital preservation in order to comply with applicable legal and regulatory requirements:

- Data Protection Act 1998;
- Freedom of Information Act 2000;

---

[6] 8 years has been specified as the typical life of electronic storage technology. This time period may be varied where technology life is estimated to be at variance with this figure.

- Environmental Information Regulations 2004;
- Money Laundering Regulations 2003;
- *add/delete all those applicable (or cross-reference alternative documentation).*

4. Document retention

This policy requires that XYZ Limited shall maintain a comprehensive Information Retention Schedule. This Schedule shall be made available as a separate document and shall be maintained by the XYZ Limited Records Manager, in compliance with the information strategy.

5. Archive model

This policy requires that an archival model for electronic information shall be maintained and implemented within the company. This archival model shall include (or shall reference) at least the following:

- procedures for the ingestion (e.g. capture) of information into the system;
- the storage strategy (see Clauses 6 and 7);

- technology maintenance and upgrade policies;
- procedures for the retrieval of information as required.

6. Storage media

This policy requires that a strategy for an appropriate storage medium (or media) is established and maintained by the Information Technology Director.

7. File formats

This policy requires that a strategy for the selection of file formats within the electronic archive model is established and implemented in accordance with the scope of this policy.

The file format selection policy shall require:

- that all information stored in an electronic form that is within the scope of this policy (see Clause 2) shall be stored in a format that conforms to the appropriate version of the ISO 19005 (use of PDF/A) series of standards;
- optionally, that information may also be stored in its native format, or in an industry standard information exchange format;

- that information stored in the ISO 19005 format shall be considered as the master record for retention purposes.

8. Metadata standards

This policy requires that appropriate metadata shall be retained in association with all stored information. Metadata models shall be agreed between the Information Owner and the Records Manager.

9. Responsibilities

The assessment of and maintenance of compliance with this policy are the responsibility of the Records Manager.

10. Preservation planning

This policy shall be reviewed annually under the control of the Records Manager.

This policy and any revisions shall be approved by the Board of Directors of XYZ Limited prior to its implementation.

Where changes are agreed, they shall be implemented using the change control procedures.